YOUR ROADMAP
TO ACADEMIC
SUCCESS

COGNICHRONICLE

ACADEMIC PLANNER
2024 - 2025

IF FOUND PLEASE RETURN TO:

ABOUT ME

NAME

BIRTHDAY

DAY		YEAR	
JAN	FEB	MAR	APR
MAY	JUN	JUL	AUG
SEP	OCT	NOV	DEC

SELF-PORTRAIT

ADDRESS

ZIP CODE

PHONE

EMAIL

SCHOOL / COLLEGE

ZIP CODE

PHONE

EMAIL

DOCTOR

DOCTOR'S OFFICE

ZIP CODE

PHONE

ALLERGIES

EMERGENCY CONTACT

RELATIONSHIP

ADDRESS

ZIP CODE

PHONE

ADDITIONAL THINGS TO NOTE

MY SCHEDULE

FROM ________ TO ________

SEMESTER ____________

TIME	MON	TUE	WED	THU	FRI

NOTES

MY SCHEDULE

FROM ________ TO ________

SEMESTER ____________

TIME	MON	TUE	WED	THU	FRI

NOTES

MY DEADLINES

ASSIGNMENTS, TESTS AND GRADE TRACKING

DATE/ TIME	CLASS	ASSIGNMENT

NOTES/FEEDBACK	☺	GRADE
	☺	
	☺	
	☺	
	☺	
	☺	
	☺	
	☺	
	☺	
	☺	
	☺	
	☺	
	☺	

2023

JANUARY

SU	MO	TU	WE	TH	FR	SA
1	2	3	4	5	6	7
8	9	10	11	12	13	14
15	16	17	18	19	20	21
22	23	24	25	26	27	28
29	30	31				

FEBRUARY

SU	MO	TU	WE	TH	FR	SA
			1	2	3	4
5	6	7	8	9	10	11
12	13	14	15	16	17	18
19	20	21	22	23	24	25
26	27	28				

MARCH

SU	MO	TU	WE	TH	FR	SA
			1	2	3	4
5	6	7	8	9	10	11
12	13	14	15	16	17	18
19	20	21	22	23	24	25
26	27	28	29	30	31	

APRIL

SU	MO	TU	WE	TH	FR	SA
						1
2	3	4	5	6	7	8
9	10	11	12	13	14	15
16	17	18	19	20	21	22
23	24	25	26	27	28	29
30						

MAY

SU	MO	TU	WE	TH	FR	SA
	1	2	3	4	5	6
7	8	9	10	11	12	13
14	15	16	17	18	19	20
21	22	23	24	25	26	27
28	29	30	31			

JUNE

SU	MO	TU	WE	TH	FR	SA
				1	2	3
4	5	6	7	8	9	10
11	12	13	14	15	16	17
18	19	20	21	22	23	24
25	26	27	28	29	30	

JULY

SU	MO	TU	WE	TH	FR	SA
						1
2	3	4	5	6	7	8
9	10	11	12	13	14	15
16	17	18	19	20	21	22
23	24	25	26	27	28	29
30	31					

AUGUST

SU	MO	TU	WE	TH	FR	SA
		1	2	3	4	5
6	7	8	9	10	11	12
13	14	15	16	17	18	19
20	21	22	23	24	25	26
27	28	29	30	31		

SEPTEMBER

SU	MO	TU	WE	TH	FR	SA
					1	2
3	4	5	6	7	8	9
10	11	12	13	14	15	16
17	18	19	20	21	22	23
24	25	26	27	28	29	30

OCTOBER

SU	MO	TU	WE	TH	FR	SA
1	2	3	4	5	6	7
8	9	10	11	12	13	14
15	16	17	18	19	20	21
22	23	24	25	26	27	28
29	30	31				

NOVEMBER

SU	MO	TU	WE	TH	FR	SA
			1	2	3	4
5	6	7	8	9	10	11
12	13	14	15	16	17	18
19	20	21	22	23	24	25
26	27	28	29	30		

DECEMBER

SU	MO	TU	WE	TH	FR	SA
					1	2
3	4	5	6	7	8	9
10	11	12	13	14	15	16
17	18	19	20	21	22	23
24	25	26	27	28	29	30
31						

2024

JANUARY

SU	MO	TU	WE	TH	FR	SA
	1	2	3	4	5	6
7	8	9	10	11	12	13
14	15	16	17	18	19	20
21	22	23	24	25	26	27
28	29	30	31			

FEBRUARY

SU	MO	TU	WE	TH	FR	SA
				1	2	3
4	5	6	7	8	9	10
11	12	13	14	15	16	17
18	19	20	21	22	23	24
25	26	27	28	29		

MARCH

SU	MO	TU	WE	TH	FR	SA
					1	2
3	4	5	6	7	8	9
10	11	12	13	14	15	16
17	18	19	20	21	22	23
24	25	26	27	28	29	30
31						

APRIL

SU	MO	TU	WE	TH	FR	SA
	1	2	3	4	5	6
7	8	9	10	11	12	13
14	15	16	17	18	19	20
21	22	23	24	25	26	27
28	29	30				

MAY

SU	MO	TU	WE	TH	FR	SA
			1	2	3	4
5	6	7	8	9	10	11
12	13	14	15	16	17	18
19	20	21	22	23	24	25
26	27	28	29	30	31	

JUNE

SU	MO	TU	WE	TH	FR	SA
						1
2	3	4	5	6	7	8
9	10	11	12	13	14	15
16	17	18	19	20	21	22
23	24	25	26	27	28	29
30						

JULY

SU	MO	TU	WE	TH	FR	SA
	1	2	3	4	5	6
7	8	9	10	11	12	13
14	15	16	17	18	19	20
21	22	23	24	25	26	27
28	29	30	31			

AUGUST

SU	MO	TU	WE	TH	FR	SA
				1	2	3
4	5	6	7	8	9	10
11	12	13	14	15	16	17
18	19	20	21	22	23	24
25	26	27	28	29	30	31

SEPTEMBER

SU	MO	TU	WE	TH	FR	SA
1	2	3	4	5	6	7
8	9	10	11	12	13	14
15	16	17	18	19	20	21
22	23	24	25	26	27	28
29	30					

OCTOBER

SU	MO	TU	WE	TH	FR	SA
		1	2	3	4	5
6	7	8	9	10	11	12
13	14	15	16	17	18	19
20	21	22	23	24	25	26
27	28	29	30	31		

NOVEMBER

SU	MO	TU	WE	TH	FR	SA
					1	2
3	4	5	6	7	8	9
10	11	12	13	14	15	16
17	18	19	20	21	22	23
24	25	26	27	28	29	30

DECEMBER

SU	MO	TU	WE	TH	FR	SA
1	2	3	4	5	6	7
8	9	10	11	12	13	14
15	16	17	18	19	20	21
22	23	24	25	26	27	28
29	30	31				

SEMESTER 1

"Success is not final, failure is not fatal: It is the courage to continue that counts."

\- Winston Churchill

INTRODUCTION TO SEMESTER 1

THIS SEMESTER'S GOALS

THIS SEMESTER'S FOCUS

MONTH OF: ____________________

SUNDAY	MONDAY	TUESDAY	WEDNESDAY

THURSDAY	FRIDAY	SATURDAY	NOTES

________________ OVERVIEW

GOALS	OBJECTIVES

MONTH OF: ____________

____ - MONDAY	____ - TUESDAY	____ - WEDNESDAY
BREAKFAST	BREAKFAST	BREAKFAST
STUDY SESSION	STUDY SESSION	STUDY SESSION
CLASS NOTES REVIEW	CLASS NOTES REVIEW	CLASS NOTES REVIEW

"Productivity is turning your intentions into actions, making progress one step at a time."

____ - THURSDAY	____ - FRIDAY	____ - SATURDAY
BREAKFAST	BREAKFAST	
		____ - SUNDAY
STUDY SESSION	STUDY SESSION	
CLASS NOTES REVIEW	CLASS NOTES REVIEW	WEEKLY REFLECTION
		GOAL ADJUSTMENT

MONTH OF: ______________

WEEK 2 OF MONTH 1

____ - MONDAY	____ - TUESDAY	____ - WEDNESDAY
STUDY GOALS	STUDY GOALS	STUDY GOALS
TASKS	TASKS	TASKS
REFLECTION	REFLECTION	REFLECTION

____ - THURSDAY

STUDY GOALS

TASKS

REFLECTION

____ - FRIDAY

STUDY GOALS

TASKS

REFLECTION

____ - SATURDAY

____ - SUNDAY

WEEKLY REFLECTION

GOAL ADJUSTMENT

MONTH OF: ______________

____ - MONDAY	____ - TUESDAY	____ - WEDNESDAY
BREAKFAST	BREAKFAST	BREAKFAST
STUDY SESSION	STUDY SESSION	STUDY SESSION
CLASS NOTES REVIEW	CLASS NOTES REVIEW	CLASS NOTES REVIEW

"Productivity is turning your intentions into actions, making progress one step at a time."

____ - THURSDAY	____ - FRIDAY	____ - SATURDAY
BREAKFAST	BREAKFAST	
		____ - SUNDAY
STUDY SESSION	STUDY SESSION	
		WEEKLY REFLECTION
CLASS NOTES REVIEW	CLASS NOTES REVIEW	
		GOAL ADJUSTMENT

MONTH OF: ____________

WEEK 4 OF MONTH 1

____ - MONDAY	____ - TUESDAY	____ - WEDNESDAY
STUDY GOALS	STUDY GOALS	STUDY GOALS
TASKS	TASKS	TASKS
REFLECTION	REFLECTION	REFLECTION

____ - THURSDAY

STUDY GOALS

TASKS

REFLECTION

____ - FRIDAY

STUDY GOALS

TASKS

REFLECTION

____ - SATURDAY

____ - SUNDAY

WEEKLY REFLECTION

GOAL ADJUSTMENT

MONTH OF: ____________________

SUNDAY	MONDAY	TUESDAY	WEDNESDAY

THURSDAY	FRIDAY	SATURDAY	NOTES

________________ OVERVIEW

GOALS

OBJECTIVES

MONTH OF: ______________

____ - MONDAY	____ - TUESDAY	____ - WEDNESDAY
BREAKFAST	BREAKFAST	BREAKFAST
STUDY SESSION	STUDY SESSION	STUDY SESSION
CLASS NOTES REVIEW	CLASS NOTES REVIEW	CLASS NOTES REVIEW

"Productivity is turning your intentions into actions, making progress one step at a time."

____ - THURSDAY	____ - FRIDAY	____ - SATURDAY
BREAKFAST	BREAKFAST	
STUDY SESSION	STUDY SESSION	____ - SUNDAY
CLASS NOTES REVIEW	CLASS NOTES REVIEW	WEEKLY REFLECTION
		GOAL ADJUSTMENT

MONTH OF: ____________

WEEK 2 OF MONTH 2

____ - MONDAY	____ - TUESDAY	____ - WEDNESDAY
STUDY GOALS	STUDY GOALS	STUDY GOALS
TASKS	TASKS	TASKS
REFLECTION	REFLECTION	REFLECTION

____ - THURSDAY	____ - FRIDAY	____ - SATURDAY
STUDY GOALS	STUDY GOALS	
		____ - SUNDAY
TASKS	TASKS	
		WEEKLY REFLECTION
REFLECTION	REFLECTION	
		GOAL ADJUSTMENT

MONTH OF: ______________

WEEK 3 OF MONTH 2

____ - MONDAY	____ - TUESDAY	____ - WEDNESDAY
BREAKFAST	BREAKFAST	BREAKFAST
STUDY SESSION	STUDY SESSION	STUDY SESSION
CLASS NOTES REVIEW	CLASS NOTES REVIEW	CLASS NOTES REVIEW

"Productivity is turning your intentions into actions, making progress one step at a time."

____ - THURSDAY

BREAKFAST

STUDY SESSION

CLASS NOTES REVIEW

____ - FRIDAY

BREAKFAST

STUDY SESSION

CLASS NOTES REVIEW

____ - SATURDAY

____ - SUNDAY

WEEKLY REFLECTION

GOAL ADJUSTMENT

MONTH OF: ____________

WEEK 4 OF MONTH 2

____ - MONDAY	____ - TUESDAY	____ - WEDNESDAY
STUDY GOALS	STUDY GOALS	STUDY GOALS
TASKS	TASKS	TASKS
REFLECTION	REFLECTION	REFLECTION

____ - THURSDAY

STUDY GOALS

TASKS

REFLECTION

____ - FRIDAY

STUDY GOALS

TASKS

REFLECTION

____ - SATURDAY

____ - SUNDAY

WEEKLY REFLECTION

GOAL ADJUSTMENT

MONTH OF: ________________

SUNDAY	MONDAY	TUESDAY	WEDNESDAY

THURSDAY	FRIDAY	SATURDAY	NOTES

________________ OVERVIEW

GOALS	OBJECTIVES

MONTH OF: ____________

____ - MONDAY

BREAKFAST

STUDY SESSION

CLASS NOTES REVIEW

____ - TUESDAY

BREAKFAST

STUDY SESSION

CLASS NOTES REVIEW

____ - WEDNESDAY

BREAKFAST

STUDY SESSION

CLASS NOTES REVIEW

"Productivity is turning your intentions into actions, making progress one step at a time."

____ - THURSDAY

BREAKFAST

STUDY SESSION

CLASS NOTES REVIEW

____ - FRIDAY

BREAKFAST

STUDY SESSION

CLASS NOTES REVIEW

____ - SATURDAY

____ - SUNDAY

WEEKLY REFLECTION

GOAL ADJUSTMENT

MONTH OF: ____________

WEEK 2 OF MONTH 3

____ - MONDAY	____ - TUESDAY	____ - WEDNESDAY
STUDY GOALS	STUDY GOALS	STUDY GOALS
TASKS	TASKS	TASKS
REFLECTION	REFLECTION	REFLECTION

____ - THURSDAY

STUDY GOALS

TASKS

REFLECTION

____ - FRIDAY

STUDY GOALS

TASKS

REFLECTION

____ - SATURDAY

____ - SUNDAY

WEEKLY REFLECTION

GOAL ADJUSTMENT

MONTH OF: ____________

WEEK 3 OF MONTH 3

____ - MONDAY	____ - TUESDAY	____ - WEDNESDAY
BREAKFAST	BREAKFAST	BREAKFAST
STUDY SESSION	STUDY SESSION	STUDY SESSION
CLASS NOTES REVIEW	CLASS NOTES REVIEW	CLASS NOTES REVIEW

"Productivity is turning your intentions into actions, making progress one step at a time."

____ - THURSDAY	____ - FRIDAY	____ - SATURDAY
BREAKFAST	BREAKFAST	
STUDY SESSION	STUDY SESSION	____ - SUNDAY
CLASS NOTES REVIEW	CLASS NOTES REVIEW	WEEKLY REFLECTION
		GOAL ADJUSTMENT

MONTH OF: ____________

WEEK 4 OF MONTH 3

____ - MONDAY	____ - TUESDAY	____ - WEDNESDAY
STUDY GOALS	STUDY GOALS	STUDY GOALS
TASKS	TASKS	TASKS
REFLECTION	REFLECTION	REFLECTION

____ - THURSDAY

STUDY GOALS

TASKS

REFLECTION

____ - FRIDAY

STUDY GOALS

TASKS

REFLECTION

____ - SATURDAY

____ - SUNDAY

WEEKLY REFLECTION

GOAL ADJUSTMENT

MONTH OF: ______________________

SUNDAY	MONDAY	TUESDAY	WEDNESDAY

THURSDAY	FRIDAY	SATURDAY	NOTES

____________________ OVERVIEW

GOALS

OBJECTIVES

MONTH OF: ______________

WEEK 1 OF MONTH 4

____ - MONDAY	____ - TUESDAY	____ - WEDNESDAY
BREAKFAST	BREAKFAST	BREAKFAST
STUDY SESSION	STUDY SESSION	STUDY SESSION
CLASS NOTES REVIEW	CLASS NOTES REVIEW	CLASS NOTES REVIEW

"Productivity is turning your intentions into actions, making progress one step at a time."

____ - THURSDAY	____ - FRIDAY	____ - SATURDAY
BREAKFAST	BREAKFAST	
		____ - SUNDAY
STUDY SESSION	STUDY SESSION	
		WEEKLY REFLECTION
CLASS NOTES REVIEW	CLASS NOTES REVIEW	
		GOAL ADJUSTMENT

MONTH OF: _______________

WEEK 2 OF MONTH 4

____ - MONDAY	____ - TUESDAY	____ - WEDNESDAY
STUDY GOALS	STUDY GOALS	STUDY GOALS
TASKS	TASKS	TASKS
REFLECTION	REFLECTION	REFLECTION

____ - THURSDAY	____ - FRIDAY	____ - SATURDAY
STUDY GOALS	STUDY GOALS	
TASKS	TASKS	____ - SUNDAY
REFLECTION	REFLECTION	WEEKLY REFLECTION
		GOAL ADJUSTMENT

MONTH OF: ______________

WEEK 3 OF MONTH 4

____ - MONDAY	____ - TUESDAY	____ - WEDNESDAY
BREAKFAST	BREAKFAST	BREAKFAST
STUDY SESSION	STUDY SESSION	STUDY SESSION
CLASS NOTES REVIEW	CLASS NOTES REVIEW	CLASS NOTES REVIEW

"Productivity is turning your intentions into actions, making progress one step at a time."

____ - THURSDAY	____ - FRIDAY	____ - SATURDAY
BREAKFAST	BREAKFAST	
STUDY SESSION	STUDY SESSION	____ - SUNDAY
CLASS NOTES REVIEW	CLASS NOTES REVIEW	WEEKLY REFLECTION
		GOAL ADJUSTMENT

MONTH OF: ____________

WEEK 4 OF MONTH 4

____ - MONDAY	____ - TUESDAY	____ - WEDNESDAY
STUDY GOALS	STUDY GOALS	STUDY GOALS
TASKS	TASKS	TASKS
REFLECTION	REFLECTION	REFLECTION

____ - THURSDAY

STUDY GOALS

TASKS

REFLECTION

____ - FRIDAY

STUDY GOALS

TASKS

REFLECTION

____ - SATURDAY

____ - SUNDAY

WEEKLY REFLECTION

GOAL ADJUSTMENT

MONTH OF: ____________________

SUNDAY	MONDAY	TUESDAY	WEDNESDAY

THURSDAY	FRIDAY	SATURDAY	NOTES

______________ OVERVIEW

GOALS

OBJECTIVES

MONTH OF: ______________

____ - MONDAY	____ - TUESDAY	____ - WEDNESDAY
BREAKFAST	BREAKFAST	BREAKFAST
STUDY SESSION	STUDY SESSION	STUDY SESSION
CLASS NOTES REVIEW	CLASS NOTES REVIEW	CLASS NOTES REVIEW

"Productivity is turning your intentions into actions, making progress one step at a time."

____ - THURSDAY	____ - FRIDAY	____ - SATURDAY
BREAKFAST	BREAKFAST	
STUDY SESSION	STUDY SESSION	____ - SUNDAY
CLASS NOTES REVIEW	CLASS NOTES REVIEW	WEEKLY REFLECTION
		GOAL ADJUSTMENT

MONTH OF: ____________

WEEK 2 OF MONTH 5

____ - MONDAY	____ - TUESDAY	____ - WEDNESDAY
STUDY GOALS	STUDY GOALS	STUDY GOALS
TASKS	TASKS	TASKS
REFLECTION	REFLECTION	REFLECTION

____ - THURSDAY	____ - FRIDAY	____ - SATURDAY
STUDY GOALS	STUDY GOALS	
TASKS	TASKS	____ - SUNDAY
REFLECTION	REFLECTION	WEEKLY REFLECTION
		GOAL ADJUSTMENT

MONTH OF: ______________

____ - MONDAY	____ - TUESDAY	____ - WEDNESDAY
BREAKFAST	BREAKFAST	BREAKFAST
STUDY SESSION	STUDY SESSION	STUDY SESSION
CLASS NOTES REVIEW	CLASS NOTES REVIEW	CLASS NOTES REVIEW

"Productivity is turning your intentions into actions, making progress one step at a time."

____ - THURSDAY	____ - FRIDAY	____ - SATURDAY
BREAKFAST	BREAKFAST	
STUDY SESSION	STUDY SESSION	____ - SUNDAY
CLASS NOTES REVIEW	CLASS NOTES REVIEW	WEEKLY REFLECTION GOAL ADJUSTMENT

MONTH OF: ______________

____ - MONDAY	____ - TUESDAY	____ - WEDNESDAY
STUDY GOALS	STUDY GOALS	STUDY GOALS
TASKS	TASKS	TASKS
REFLECTION	REFLECTION	REFLECTION

____ - THURSDAY

STUDY GOALS

TASKS

REFLECTION

____ - FRIDAY

STUDY GOALS

TASKS

REFLECTION

____ - SATURDAY

____ - SUNDAY

WEEKLY REFLECTION

GOAL ADJUSTMENT

REFLECT & REFINE

ACCOMPLISHMENTS

IMPROVEMENTS FOR THE SEMESTER

CHALLENGES

SEMESTER 1 – SELF REWARD

WRITE A NOTE TO YOURSELF FOR COMPLETING THE SEMESTER

STUDY SESSIONS & REWARDS

CHECK A BOX FOR EACH COMPLETED STUDY SESSION, AND CLAIM REWARDS AS YOU EARN THEM.

DATE	STUDY SUBJECT	COMPLETED
		☐
		☐
		☐
		☐
		☐
		☐
		☐
		☐
		☐
		☐
		☐
		☐

REWARDS	
☐	FREE TIME: Allowing yourself some guilt-free leisure time to relax and recharge is a great reward.
☐	MOVIE OR GAME NIGHT: Organize a movie or game night with friends to unwind and have fun.
☐	TREAT YOURSELF: Buy yourself a small treat or snack you've been craving.
☐	SPA OR SELF-CARE DAY: Indulge in a spa day or self-care routine to pamper yourself
☐	COOK A SPECIAL MEAL: Prepare a favorite meal or try out a new recipe you've been curious about.
☐	NEW BOOK OR MAGAZINE: Buy a new book or magazine you're interested in reading for leisure.
☐	OUTDOOR ADVENTURE: Plan a hike, picnic, or outdoor adventure to enjoy nature.
☐	ARTISTIC PURSUITS: Invest in art supplies for painting, drawing, or any other creative outlet you enjoy.
☐	VISIT A MUSEUM OR EXHIBITION: Spend a day exploring a museum or art exhibition.
☐	NEW CLOTHING ITEM: Treat yourself to a new clothing item you've been wanting.
☐	SOCIAL GATHERING: Organize a gathering with friends, like a barbecue or picnic.
☐	MUSIC PLAYLIST: Curate a new playlist with your favorite songs and discover new ones.
☐	ONLINE SHOPPING: Shop for items you've had your eye on, whether it's clothing, gadgets, or décor.
☐	LANGUAGE LEARNING: Invest time in learning a new language or practicing one you're already learning.
☐	NETWORKING EVENT: Attend a networking event related to your field of study.
☐	DAY OFF: Give yourself a full day off from responsibilities to do whatever you want.
☐	PHOTOGRAPHY DAY: Take a day to explore your surroundings and practice photography.
☐	MINDFULNESS AND MEDITATION: Dedicate time to mindfulness, meditation, or relaxation exercises.

STUDY HOURS TRACKER

FROM ________ TO ________

SEMESTER ____________

TIME	MON	TUE	WED	THU	FRI

FINANCE TRACKER

FROM ________ TO ________

SEMESTER ____________

STARTING BALANCE ________________ WEEKS TO COVER ______________

DATE	INCOME	AMOUNT
	TOTAL INCOME	

DATE	SPENDING	AMOUNT
	TOTAL SPENDING	

WEEKLY BUDGET ________________ MONTHLY BUDGET ______________

MY NOTES

RECIPE IDEAS

DISH

RECIPE

INGREDIENTS

- [ ]
- [ ]
- [ ]
- [ ]
- [ ]
- [ ]
- [ ]
- [ ]

DISH

RECIPE

INGREDIENTS

- [ ]
- [ ]
- [ ]
- [ ]
- [ ]
- [ ]
- [ ]
- [ ]

DISH

RECIPE

INGREDIENTS

- [ ]
- [ ]
- [ ]
- [ ]
- [ ]
- [ ]
- [ ]
- [ ]

BREAKFAST

DISH

RECIPE

INGREDIENTS

- [ ]
- [ ]
- [ ]
- [ ]
- [ ]
- [ ]
- [ ]
- [ ]

DISH

RECIPE

INGREDIENTS

- [ ]
- [ ]
- [ ]
- [ ]
- [ ]
- [ ]
- [ ]
- [ ]

DISH

RECIPE

INGREDIENTS

- [ ]
- [ ]
- [ ]
- [ ]
- [ ]
- [ ]
- [ ]
- [ ]

RECIPE IDEAS

DISH

RECIPE

INGREDIENTS

- [ ]
- [ ]
- [ ]
- [ ]
- [ ]
- [ ]
- [ ]
- [ ]

DISH

RECIPE

INGREDIENTS

- [ ]
- [ ]
- [ ]
- [ ]
- [ ]
- [ ]
- [ ]
- [ ]

DISH

RECIPE

INGREDIENTS

- [ ]
- [ ]
- [ ]
- [ ]
- [ ]
- [ ]
- [ ]
- [ ]

LUNCH

DISH

RECIPE

INGREDIENTS

- ☐
- ☐
- ☐
- ☐
- ☐
- ☐
- ☐
- ☐

DISH

RECIPE

INGREDIENTS

- ☐
- ☐
- ☐
- ☐
- ☐
- ☐
- ☐
- ☐

DISH

RECIPE

INGREDIENTS

- ☐
- ☐
- ☐
- ☐
- ☐
- ☐
- ☐
- ☐

SEMESTER 2

"Success is not final, failure is not fatal: It is the courage to continue that counts."
- Winston Churchill

INTRODUCTION TO SEMESTER 2

THIS SEMESTER'S GOALS

THIS SEMESTER'S FOCUS

MONTH OF: ________________

SUNDAY	MONDAY	TUESDAY	WEDNESDAY

THURSDAY	FRIDAY	SATURDAY	NOTES

_______________ OVERVIEW

GOALS

OBJECTIVES

MONTH OF: _______________

____ - MONDAY	____ - TUESDAY	____ - WEDNESDAY
BREAKFAST	BREAKFAST	BREAKFAST
STUDY SESSION	STUDY SESSION	STUDY SESSION
CLASS NOTES REVIEW	CLASS NOTES REVIEW	CLASS NOTES REVIEW

"Productivity is turning your intentions into actions, making progress one step at a time."

____ - THURSDAY	____ - FRIDAY	____ - SATURDAY
BREAKFAST	BREAKFAST	
STUDY SESSION	STUDY SESSION	____ - SUNDAY
CLASS NOTES REVIEW	CLASS NOTES REVIEW	WEEKLY REFLECTION
		GOAL ADJUSTMENT

MONTH OF: ____________

WEEK 2 OF MONTH 1

____ - MONDAY	____ - TUESDAY	____ - WEDNESDAY
STUDY GOALS	STUDY GOALS	STUDY GOALS
TASKS	TASKS	TASKS
REFLECTION	REFLECTION	REFLECTION

____ - THURSDAY

STUDY GOALS

TASKS

REFLECTION

____ - FRIDAY

STUDY GOALS

TASKS

REFLECTION

____ - SATURDAY

____ - SUNDAY

WEEKLY REFLECTION

GOAL ADJUSTMENT

MONTH OF: ______________

WEEK 3 OF MONTH 1

____ - MONDAY	____ - TUESDAY	____ - WEDNESDAY
BREAKFAST	BREAKFAST	BREAKFAST
STUDY SESSION	STUDY SESSION	STUDY SESSION
CLASS NOTES REVIEW	CLASS NOTES REVIEW	CLASS NOTES REVIEW

"Productivity is turning your intentions into actions, making progress one step at a time."

____ - THURSDAY

BREAKFAST

STUDY SESSION

CLASS NOTES REVIEW

____ - FRIDAY

BREAKFAST

STUDY SESSION

CLASS NOTES REVIEW

____ - SATURDAY

____ - SUNDAY

WEEKLY REFLECTION

GOAL ADJUSTMENT

MONTH OF: ______________

____ - MONDAY	____ - TUESDAY	____ - WEDNESDAY
STUDY GOALS	STUDY GOALS	STUDY GOALS
TASKS	TASKS	TASKS
REFLECTION	REFLECTION	REFLECTION

____ - THURSDAY

STUDY GOALS

TASKS

REFLECTION

____ - FRIDAY

STUDY GOALS

TASKS

REFLECTION

____ - SATURDAY

____ - SUNDAY

WEEKLY REFLECTION

GOAL ADJUSTMENT

MONTH OF: ____________________

SUNDAY	MONDAY	TUESDAY	WEDNESDAY

THURSDAY	FRIDAY	SATURDAY	NOTES

________________ OVERVIEW

GOALS	OBJECTIVES

MONTH OF: ____________

WEEK 1 OF MONTH 2

____ - MONDAY	____ - TUESDAY	____ - WEDNESDAY
BREAKFAST	BREAKFAST	BREAKFAST
STUDY SESSION	STUDY SESSION	STUDY SESSION
CLASS NOTES REVIEW	CLASS NOTES REVIEW	CLASS NOTES REVIEW

"Productivity is turning your intentions into actions, making progress one step at a time."

____ - THURSDAY	____ - FRIDAY	____ - SATURDAY
BREAKFAST	BREAKFAST	
		____ - SUNDAY
STUDY SESSION	STUDY SESSION	
		WEEKLY REFLECTION
CLASS NOTES REVIEW	CLASS NOTES REVIEW	
		GOAL ADJUSTMENT

MONTH OF: ____________

WEEK 2 OF MONTH 2

____ - MONDAY	____ - TUESDAY	____ - WEDNESDAY
STUDY GOALS	STUDY GOALS	STUDY GOALS
TASKS	TASKS	TASKS
REFLECTION	REFLECTION	REFLECTION

____ - THURSDAY	____ - FRIDAY	____ - SATURDAY
STUDY GOALS	STUDY GOALS	
TASKS	TASKS	____ - SUNDAY
REFLECTION	REFLECTION	WEEKLY REFLECTION
		GOAL ADJUSTMENT

MONTH OF: ______________

WEEK 3 OF MONTH 2

____ - MONDAY	____ - TUESDAY	____ - WEDNESDAY
BREAKFAST	BREAKFAST	BREAKFAST
STUDY SESSION	STUDY SESSION	STUDY SESSION
CLASS NOTES REVIEW	CLASS NOTES REVIEW	CLASS NOTES REVIEW

"Productivity is turning your intentions into actions, making progress one step at a time."

____ - THURSDAY

BREAKFAST

STUDY SESSION

CLASS NOTES REVIEW

____ - FRIDAY

BREAKFAST

STUDY SESSION

CLASS NOTES REVIEW

____ - SATURDAY

____ - SUNDAY

WEEKLY REFLECTION

GOAL ADJUSTMENT

MONTH OF: ____________

WEEK 4 OF MONTH 2

____ - MONDAY	____ - TUESDAY	____ - WEDNESDAY
STUDY GOALS	STUDY GOALS	STUDY GOALS
TASKS	TASKS	TASKS
REFLECTION	REFLECTION	REFLECTION

____ - THURSDAY

STUDY GOALS

TASKS

REFLECTION

____ - FRIDAY

STUDY GOALS

TASKS

REFLECTION

____ - SATURDAY

____ - SUNDAY

WEEKLY REFLECTION

GOAL ADJUSTMENT

MONTH OF: ____________________

SUNDAY	MONDAY	TUESDAY	WEDNESDAY

THURSDAY	FRIDAY	SATURDAY	NOTES

______________ OVERVIEW

GOALS	OBJECTIVES

MONTH OF: ____________

____ - MONDAY	____ - TUESDAY	____ - WEDNESDAY
BREAKFAST	BREAKFAST	BREAKFAST
STUDY SESSION	STUDY SESSION	STUDY SESSION
CLASS NOTES REVIEW	CLASS NOTES REVIEW	CLASS NOTES REVIEW

"Productivity is turning your intentions into actions, making progress one step at a time."

____ - THURSDAY

BREAKFAST

STUDY SESSION

CLASS NOTES REVIEW

____ - FRIDAY

BREAKFAST

STUDY SESSION

CLASS NOTES REVIEW

____ - SATURDAY

____ - SUNDAY

WEEKLY REFLECTION

GOAL ADJUSTMENT

MONTH OF: ____________

____ - MONDAY	____ - TUESDAY	____ - WEDNESDAY
STUDY GOALS	STUDY GOALS	STUDY GOALS
TASKS	TASKS	TASKS
REFLECTION	REFLECTION	REFLECTION

____ - THURSDAY

STUDY GOALS

TASKS

REFLECTION

____ - FRIDAY

STUDY GOALS

TASKS

REFLECTION

____ - SATURDAY

____ - SUNDAY

WEEKLY REFLECTION

GOAL ADJUSTMENT

MONTH OF: ____________

____ - MONDAY	____ - TUESDAY	____ - WEDNESDAY
BREAKFAST	BREAKFAST	BREAKFAST
STUDY SESSION	STUDY SESSION	STUDY SESSION
CLASS NOTES REVIEW	CLASS NOTES REVIEW	CLASS NOTES REVIEW

"Productivity is turning your intentions into actions, making progress one step at a time."

____ - THURSDAY

BREAKFAST

STUDY SESSION

CLASS NOTES REVIEW

____ - FRIDAY

BREAKFAST

STUDY SESSION

CLASS NOTES REVIEW

____ - SATURDAY

____ - SUNDAY

WEEKLY REFLECTION

GOAL ADJUSTMENT

MONTH OF: ____________

WEEK 4 OF MONTH 3

____ - MONDAY	____ - TUESDAY	____ - WEDNESDAY
STUDY GOALS	STUDY GOALS	STUDY GOALS
TASKS	TASKS	TASKS
REFLECTION	REFLECTION	REFLECTION

____ - THURSDAY	____ - FRIDAY	____ - SATURDAY
STUDY GOALS	STUDY GOALS	
TASKS	TASKS	____ - SUNDAY
REFLECTION	REFLECTION	WEEKLY REFLECTION
		GOAL ADJUSTMENT

MONTH OF: ______________________

SUNDAY	MONDAY	TUESDAY	WEDNESDAY

THURSDAY	FRIDAY	SATURDAY	NOTES

______________ OVERVIEW

GOALS

OBJECTIVES

MONTH OF: ____________

WEEK 1 OF MONTH 4

____ - MONDAY	____ - TUESDAY	____ - WEDNESDAY
BREAKFAST	BREAKFAST	BREAKFAST
STUDY SESSION	STUDY SESSION	STUDY SESSION
CLASS NOTES REVIEW	CLASS NOTES REVIEW	CLASS NOTES REVIEW

"Productivity is turning your intentions into actions, making progress one step at a time."

____ - THURSDAY	____ - FRIDAY	____ - SATURDAY
BREAKFAST	BREAKFAST	
STUDY SESSION	STUDY SESSION	____ - SUNDAY
CLASS NOTES REVIEW	CLASS NOTES REVIEW	WEEKLY REFLECTION
		GOAL ADJUSTMENT

MONTH OF: ____________

WEEK 2 OF MONTH 4

____ - MONDAY	____ - TUESDAY	____ - WEDNESDAY
STUDY GOALS	STUDY GOALS	STUDY GOALS
TASKS	TASKS	TASKS
REFLECTION	REFLECTION	REFLECTION

____ - THURSDAY

STUDY GOALS

TASKS

REFLECTION

____ - FRIDAY

STUDY GOALS

TASKS

REFLECTION

____ - SATURDAY

____ - SUNDAY

WEEKLY REFLECTION

GOAL ADJUSTMENT

MONTH OF: ____________

WEEK 3 OF MONTH 4

____ - MONDAY	____ - TUESDAY	____ - WEDNESDAY
BREAKFAST	BREAKFAST	BREAKFAST
STUDY SESSION	STUDY SESSION	STUDY SESSION
CLASS NOTES REVIEW	CLASS NOTES REVIEW	CLASS NOTES REVIEW

"Productivity is turning your intentions into actions, making progress one step at a time."

____ - THURSDAY	____ - FRIDAY	____ - SATURDAY
BREAKFAST	BREAKFAST	
STUDY SESSION	STUDY SESSION	____ - SUNDAY
CLASS NOTES REVIEW	CLASS NOTES REVIEW	WEEKLY REFLECTION
		GOAL ADJUSTMENT

MONTH OF: ____________

WEEK 4 OF MONTH 4

____ - MONDAY	____ - TUESDAY	____ - WEDNESDAY
STUDY GOALS	STUDY GOALS	STUDY GOALS
TASKS	TASKS	TASKS
REFLECTION	REFLECTION	REFLECTION

____ - THURSDAY

STUDY GOALS

TASKS

REFLECTION

____ - FRIDAY

STUDY GOALS

TASKS

REFLECTION

____ - SATURDAY

____ - SUNDAY

WEEKLY REFLECTION

GOAL ADJUSTMENT

MONTH OF: ____________________

SUNDAY	MONDAY	TUESDAY	WEDNESDAY

THURSDAY	FRIDAY	SATURDAY	NOTES

________________ OVERVIEW

GOALS

OBJECTIVES

MONTH OF: ______________

____ - MONDAY	____ - TUESDAY	____ - WEDNESDAY
BREAKFAST	BREAKFAST	BREAKFAST
STUDY SESSION	STUDY SESSION	STUDY SESSION
CLASS NOTES REVIEW	CLASS NOTES REVIEW	

"Productivity is turning your intentions into actions, making progress one step at a time."

____ - THURSDAY

BREAKFAST

STUDY SESSION

CLASS NOTES REVIEW

____ - FRIDAY

BREAKFAST

STUDY SESSION

CLASS NOTES REVIEW

____ - SATURDAY

____ - SUNDAY

WEEKLY REFLECTION

GOAL ADJUSTMENT

MONTH OF: ______________

WEEK 2 OF MONTH 5

____ - MONDAY

STUDY GOALS

TASKS

REFLECTION

____ - TUESDAY

STUDY GOALS

TASKS

REFLECTION

____ - WEDNESDAY

STUDY GOALS

TASKS

REF

_______________ OVERVIEW

GOALS	OBJECTIVES

MONTH OF: ______________

____ - MONDAY	____ - TUESDAY	____ - WEDNESDAY
BREAKFAST	BREAKFAST	BREAKFAST
STUDY SESSION	STUDY SESSION	STUDY SESSION
CLASS NOTES REVIEW	CLASS NOTES REVIEW	CLASS NOTES REVIEW

"Productivity is turning your intentions into actions, making progress one step at a time."

____ - THURSDAY	____ - FRIDAY	____ - SATURDAY
BREAKFAST	BREAKFAST	
STUDY SESSION	STUDY SESSION	____ - SUNDAY
CLASS NOTES REVIEW	CLASS NOTES REVIEW	WEEKLY REFLECTION
		GOAL ADJUSTMENT

MONTH OF: ____________

WEEK 2 OF MONTH 5

____ - MONDAY	____ - TUESDAY	____ - WEDNESDAY
STUDY GOALS	STUDY GOALS	STUDY GOALS
TASKS	TASKS	TASKS
REFLECTION	REFLECTION	REFLECTION

____ - THURSDAY	____ - FRIDAY	____ - SATURDAY
STUDY GOALS	STUDY GOALS	
TASKS	TASKS	____ - SUNDAY
REFLECTION	REFLECTION	WEEKLY REFLECTION
		GOAL ADJUSTMENT

MONTH OF: ____________

____ - MONDAY	____ - TUESDAY	____ - WEDNESDAY
BREAKFAST	BREAKFAST	BREAKFAST
STUDY SESSION	STUDY SESSION	STUDY SESSION
CLASS NOTES REVIEW	CLASS NOTES REVIEW	CLASS NOTES REVIEW

"Productivity is turning your intentions into actions, making progress one step at a time."

____ - THURSDAY	____ - FRIDAY	____ - SATURDAY
BREAKFAST	BREAKFAST	
STUDY SESSION	STUDY SESSION	____ - SUNDAY
CLASS NOTES REVIEW	CLASS NOTES REVIEW	WEEKLY REFLECTION
		GOAL ADJUSTMENT

MONTH OF: ______________

WEEK 4 OF MONTH 5

____ - MONDAY	____ - TUESDAY	____ - WEDNESDAY
STUDY GOALS	STUDY GOALS	STUDY GOALS
TASKS	TASKS	TASKS
REFLECTION	REFLECTION	REFLECTION

____ - THURSDAY	____ - FRIDAY	____ - SATURDAY
STUDY GOALS	STUDY GOALS	
TASKS	TASKS	____ - SUNDAY
		WEEKLY REFLECTION
REFLECTION	REFLECTION	GOAL ADJUSTMENT

MONTH OF: ____________________

SUNDAY	MONDAY	TUESDAY	WEDNESDAY

THURSDAY	FRIDAY	SATURDAY	NOTES

________________ OVERVIEW

GOALS	OBJECTIVES

MONTH OF: ______________

WEEK 1 OF MONTH 6

____ - MONDAY	____ - TUESDAY	____ - WEDNESDAY
BREAKFAST	BREAKFAST	BREAKFAST
STUDY SESSION	STUDY SESSION	STUDY SESSION
CLASS NOTES REVIEW	CLASS NOTES REVIEW	CLASS NOTES REVIEW

"Productivity is turning your intentions into actions, making progress one step at a time."

____ - THURSDAY

BREAKFAST

STUDY SESSION

CLASS NOTES REVIEW

____ - FRIDAY

BREAKFAST

STUDY SESSION

CLASS NOTES REVIEW

____ - SATURDAY

____ - SUNDAY

WEEKLY REFLECTION

GOAL ADJUSTMENT

MONTH OF: ______________

WEEK 2 OF MONTH 6

____ - MONDAY	____ - TUESDAY	____ - WEDNESDAY
STUDY GOALS	STUDY GOALS	STUDY GOALS
TASKS	TASKS	TASKS
REFLECTION	REFLECTION	REFLECTION

____ - THURSDAY

STUDY GOALS

TASKS

REFLECTION

____ - FRIDAY

STUDY GOALS

TASKS

REFLECTION

____ - SATURDAY

____ - SUNDAY

WEEKLY REFLECTION

GOAL ADJUSTMENT

MONTH OF: ______________

WEEK 3 OF MONTH 6

____ - MONDAY	____ - TUESDAY	____ - WEDNESDAY
BREAKFAST	BREAKFAST	BREAKFAST
STUDY SESSION	STUDY SESSION	STUDY SESSION
CLASS NOTES REVIEW	CLASS NOTES REVIEW	CLASS NOTES REVIEW

"Productivity is turning your intentions into actions, making progress one step at a time."

____ - THURSDAY

BREAKFAST

STUDY SESSION

CLASS NOTES REVIEW

____ - FRIDAY

BREAKFAST

STUDY SESSION

CLASS NOTES REVIEW

____ - SATURDAY

____ - SUNDAY

WEEKLY REFLECTION

GOAL ADJUSTMENT

MONTH OF: ______________

WEEK 4 OF MONTH 6

____ - MONDAY	____ - TUESDAY	____ - WEDNESDAY
STUDY GOALS	STUDY GOALS	STUDY GOALS
TASKS	TASKS	TASKS
REFLECTION	REFLECTION	REFLECTION

____ - THURSDAY

STUDY GOALS

TASKS

REFLECTION

____ - FRIDAY

STUDY GOALS

TASKS

REFLECTION

____ - SATURDAY

____ - SUNDAY

WEEKLY REFLECTION

GOAL ADJUSTMENT

REFLECT & REFINE

ACCOMPLISHMENTS

IMPROVEMENTS FOR THE SEMESTER

CHALLENGES

SEMESTER 2 – SELF REWARD

WRITE A NOTE TO YOURSELF FOR COMPLETING THE SEMESTER

STUDY SESSIONS & REWARDS

CHECK A BOX FOR EACH COMPLETED STUDY SESSION, AND CLAIM REWARDS AS YOU EARN THEM.

DATE	STUDY SUBJECT	COMPLETED
		☐
		☐
		☐
		☐
		☐
		☐
		☐
		☐
		☐
		☐
		☐
		☐

REWARDS	
☐	**FREE TIME**: Allowing yourself some guilt-free leisure time to relax and recharge is a great reward.
☐	**MOVIE OR GAME NIGHT**: Organize a movie or game night with friends to unwind and have fun.
☐	**TREAT YOURSELF**: Buy yourself a small treat or snack you've been craving.
☐	**SPA OR SELF-CARE DAY**: Indulge in a spa day or self-care routine to pamper yourself
☐	**COOK A SPECIAL MEAL**: Prepare a favorite meal or try out a new recipe you've been curious about.
☐	**NEW BOOK OR MAGAZINE**: Buy a new book or magazine you're interested in reading for leisure.
☐	**OUTDOOR ADVENTURE**: Plan a hike, picnic, or outdoor adventure to enjoy nature.
☐	ARTISTIC PURSUITS: Invest in art supplies for painting, drawing, or any other creative outlet you enjoy.
☐	**VISIT A MUSEUM OR EXHIBITION**: Spend a day exploring a museum or art exhibition.
☐	**NEW CLOTHING ITEM**: Treat yourself to a new clothing item you've been wanting.
☐	**SOCIAL GATHERING**: Organize a gathering with friends, like a barbecue or picnic.
☐	**MUSIC PLAYLIST**: Curate a new playlist with your favorite songs and discover new ones.
☐	ONLINE SHOPPING: Shop for items you've had your eye on, whether it's clothing, gadgets, or décor.
☐	**LANGUAGE LEARNING**: Invest time in learning a new language or practicing one you're already learning.
☐	**NETWORKING EVENT**: Attend a networking event related to your field of study.
☐	**DAY OFF**: Give yourself a full day off from responsibilities to do whatever you want.
☐	**PHOTOGRAPHY DAY**: Take a day to explore your surroundings and practice photography.
☐	**MINDFULNESS AND MEDITATION**: Dedicate time to mindfulness, meditation, or relaxation exercises.

STUDY HOURS TRACKER

FROM ________ TO ________

SEMESTER ____________

TIME	MON	TUE	WED	THU	FRI

FINANCE TRACKER

FROM ________ TO ________

SEMESTER ____________

STARTING BALANCE ________________ WEEKS TO COVER ______________

DATE	INCOME	AMOUNT
	TOTAL INCOME	

DATE	SPENDING	AMOUNT
	TOTAL SPENDING	

WEEKLY BUDGET ________________ MONTHLY BUDGET ______________

MY NOTES

RECIPE IDEAS

DISH

RECIPE

INGREDIENTS

- [ ]
- [ ]
- [ ]
- [ ]
- [ ]
- [ ]
- [ ]
- [ ]

DISH

RECIPE

INGREDIENTS

- [ ]
- [ ]
- [ ]
- [ ]
- [ ]
- [ ]
- [ ]
- [ ]

DISH

RECIPE

INGREDIENTS

- [ ]
- [ ]
- [ ]
- [ ]
- [ ]
- [ ]
- [ ]
- [ ]

BREAKFAST

DISH

RECIPE

INGREDIENTS

- [ ]
- [ ]
- [ ]
- [ ]
- [ ]
- [ ]
- [ ]
- [ ]

DISH

RECIPE

INGREDIENTS

- [ ]
- [ ]
- [ ]
- [ ]
- [ ]
- [ ]
- [ ]
- [ ]

DISH

RECIPE

INGREDIENTS

- [ ]
- [ ]
- [ ]
- [ ]
- [ ]
- [ ]
- [ ]
- [ ]

RECIPE IDEAS

DISH

RECIPE

INGREDIENTS

- [ ]
- [ ]
- [ ]
- [ ]
- [ ]
- [ ]
- [ ]
- [ ]

DISH

RECIPE

INGREDIENTS

- [ ]
- [ ]
- [ ]
- [ ]
- [ ]
- [ ]
- [ ]
- [ ]

DISH

RECIPE

INGREDIENTS

- [ ]
- [ ]
- [ ]
- [ ]
- [ ]
- [ ]
- [ ]
- [ ]

LUNCH

DISH

RECIPE

INGREDIENTS

- [ ]
- [ ]
- [ ]
- [ ]
- [ ]
- [ ]
- [ ]
- [ ]

DISH

RECIPE

INGREDIENTS

- [ ]
- [ ]
- [ ]
- [ ]
- [ ]
- [ ]
- [ ]
- [ ]

DISH

RECIPE

INGREDIENTS

- [ ]
- [ ]
- [ ]
- [ ]
- [ ]
- [ ]
- [ ]
- [ ]

FINAL THOUGHTS

ENCOURAGING MESSAGE ABOUT YOUR ACADEMIC JOURNEY

CONTACT US:

"Never stop learning because life never stops teaching."

- Anonymous

Made in the USA
Monee, IL
03 November 2026

67384334R00089